SEARCH RESPONSIBLY:

The Employment Seeker's

Handbook

By

Solomon T. Adonis

TABLE OF CONTENT

DISCLAIMER

electronically, transferred, nor kept in a database. Neither in part nor full can the document be copied, scanned, faxed, or retained without approval from the publisher or creator.

INTRODUCTION

In today's dynamic job market, seeking meaningful and rewarding employment requires a strategic and informed approach. Whether you're a recent graduate or a seasoned professional, we can help you find your next career opportunity. Opportunities and navigating the complexities of job searching can be both exhilarating and daunting.

Search Responsibly: The Employment Seeker's Handbook is a comprehensive guide meticulously crafted to assist job seekers at every stage of their quest for employment. This handbook empowers you with the knowledge, tools, and strategies to navigate the job search landscape responsibly and effectively.

You'll find many insights, practical advice, and actionable steps within these pages. This handbook covers everything from understanding the nuances of today's job market to honing your resume, mastering the art of networking, excelling in interviews, and making informed decisions about job offers. Moreover, it delves into the ethical considerations and best practices that underscore a responsible job search.

The workplace is constantly changing as a result of technological advancements, consumer trends, and cultural shifts. This book aims to equip you with timeless principles and help you adapt to the changing demands and opportunities that shape the professional world. Above all, this handbook encourages you to approach your job search with mindfulness, integrity, and resilience. Each chapter is tailored to guide, emphasizing the importance of ethical conduct, self-reflection, and continuous improvement.

Embark on this journey with an open mind and a willingness to explore new strategies. Adopting a responsible and proactive approach to your job search will enhance your prospects, amplify your professional brand, and ultimately pave the way for a fulfilling career.

Welcome to *Search Responsibly: The Employment Seeker's Handbook*, where your journey toward securing meaningful employment begins.

CHAPTER 1

UNDERSTANDING THE MODERN JOB MARKET

In today's rapidly evolving job market, a profound comprehension of its dynamics is key to navigating and succeeding in your career pursuits. This chapter provides a comprehensive overview, offering insights into the contemporary professional landscape's intricacies and trends.

1.1 The Digital Transformation: Explore how technological advancements endeavor to establish new positions and open doors while transforming traditional roles. Understand the significance of digital skills and how they influence job requirements across various sectors.

1.2 Changing Industry Trends: Delve into the latest industry trends and their impact on employment. Learn how emerging fields, such as AI, renewable energy, and healthcare technology, shape job markets and where future opportunities might lie.

1.3 Gig Economy and Remote Work: Uncover the growth of remote employment and gig economy arrangements. Understand their implications for job seekers, including the flexibility they offer and the skills needed to thrive in these non-traditional work setups.

1.4 Diversity, Equity, and Inclusion: Examine the growing accentuation on variety, value, and consideration in the working environment. Learn about the importance of these values in company cultures and how job seekers can align themselves with organizations that priorities these principles.

1.5 Globalization and Market Interconnectivity: Explore how globalization has expanded job markets across borders and understand the impact of international interconnectedness on career opportunities.

1.6 Adapting to Market Changes: Strategies for staying adaptable in a constantly evolving job market. Discover how continuous learning, upskilling, and a proactive mindset can empower job seekers to thrive amidst change. This section gives a primary comprehension of the modern job landscape, equipping readers with the knowledge to make informed career decisions in an ever-shifting environment. Understanding these market dynamics will be fundamental as you progress through subsequent chapters in your quest for meaningful employment.

CHAPTER 2

BUILDING AN EFFECTIVE JOB SEARCH STRATEGY

A successful job search strategy is the cornerstone of landing the right employment opportunity. This chapter focuses on guiding job seekers through developing a comprehensive plan to maximize their chances of securing fulfilling roles.

2.1 Defining Your Goals: Understand the importance of setting clear and achievable career objectives. Learn how to align your aspirations with your skills, values, and long-term ambitions to create a roadmap for success.

2.2 Identifying Your Skills and Strengths: Conduct a self-assessment to identify your strengths, competencies, and unique selling points. Utilize tools and exercises to recognize and articulate your skills effectively to potential employers.

2.3 Crafting Your Brand: Develop a personal brand communicating your professional identity and values. Learn strategies to enhance your online presence through social media, professional networking platforms, and personal websites.

2.4 Tailoring Your Job Search Approach: Explore different job search methods and platforms that align with your career goals. Discover how to effectively leverage networking, job boards, recruitment agencies, and other resources.

2.5 Setting Priorities and Managing Time: Learn techniques for organizing and prioritizing your job search activities. Develop time management skills to maintain focus and productivity throughout the process.

2.6 Evaluating and Adjusting Your

Strategy: Understand the significance of consistently assessing the viability of your job search strategy. Learn to adapt and refine your approach based on feedback and market trends.

This chapter serves as a strategic framework to empower job seekers in creating a roadmap toward their desired career path. By understanding their goals, strengths, and utilizing effective job search techniques, readers will be better equipped to navigate the job market confidently and purposefully.

2.1 DEFINING YOUR GOALS

Setting clear and well-defined career goals is pivotal in shaping a successful job search strategy. This section provides a detailed roadmap to help individuals identify, refine, and articulate their professional aspirations.

Understanding Your Passions and Interests: Delve into introspective exercises to uncover your genuine passions and interests. Explore what motivates and excites you within your professional sphere.

Assessing Your Skills and Strengths: Conduct a comprehensive assessment of your skills, experiences, and strengths. Utilize SWOT (Strengths, Weaknesses, Opportunities, Threats) analysis to identify areas of expertise and improvement.

Clarifying Short-term and Long-term Objectives: Differentiate between short-term career objectives and long-term aspirations. Create a roadmap that outlines achievable milestones while keeping sight of the broader career trajectory.

Aligning Goals with Personal Values: Evaluate how your career goals align with your values and principles. Assessing this alignment ensures a more fulfilling and purpose-driven career path.

Setting SMART Goals: Learn the SMART criteria (Specific, Measurable, Achievable, Relevant, Time-Bound) to create concrete and achievable goals. Applying this framework ensures that your objectives are clear and actionable.

Creating a Personal Mission Statement: Craft a succinct and impactful mission statement encapsulating your career aspirations, values, and overarching purpose. This statement serves as a guiding beacon throughout your professional journey.

Seeking Mentorship and Guidance: Explore the benefits of seeking mentorship and guidance in defining your career goals. Learn how mentors can offer valuable insights and support in shaping your aspirations.

Job seekers can better understand their professional objectives by engaging in these exercises and processes. Defining these goals provides direction and focus, empowering people to tailor their pursuit of employment systems to align with their aspirations effectively.

2.2 IDENTIFYING YOUR SKILLS AND STRENGTHS

Recognizing and articulating your skills and strengths is fundamental to presenting yourself effectively in the job market. This section offers guidance on conducting a comprehensive self-assessment to identify and highlight your unique abilities.

Self-Reflection and Inventory: Conduct self-reflection exercises to identify hard and soft skills. Assess past experiences, achievements, and challenges to pinpoint skills developed in various settings.

Skills Assessment Tools: Use skills and resources to evaluate your competencies objectively. Explore online assessments, self-evaluation frameworks, or professional guidance to identify and validate your skill set.

Distinguishing Between Hard and Soft Skills: Understand the distinction between hard skills (technical abilities specific to a job) and soft skills (interpersonal, communication, leadership). Identify strengths in both categories to present a well-rounded profile.

Feedback and 360-degree Assessment: Seek feedback from peers, mentors, or former colleagues to view your strengths comprehensively. A 360-degree assessment can provide valuable insights from multiple perspectives.

Translating Experiences into Skills: Learn to translate diverse experiences, including volunteer work, hobbies, or side projects, into valuable skills applicable to the job market. Distinguish adaptable abilities that can be important in various roles or industries.

Building a Skills Inventory: Create a structured inventory or portfolio showcasing your skills, experiences, certifications, and accomplishments. This document is a reference and can be tailored for specific job applications.

Emphasizing Strengths in Applications: Effectively incorporate identified skills and strengths into resumes, cover letters, and interviews. Craft compelling narratives that highlight your unique value proposition to potential employers.

By systematically assessing and recognizing your skills and strengths, you equip yourself with the confidence and clarity to market yourself effectively to potential employers. Understanding your unique skill set enables you to strategically position yourself as an ideal candidate in the competitive job market.

2.3 CRAFTING YOUR BRAND

Developing a distinct personal brand is pivotal in leaving a lasting impression and standing out amidst the competition. This section focuses on strategies to craft and communicate a compelling personal brand that aligns with your professional goals.

Grasping Individual Marking: Investigate the idea of individual marking and its significance in today's job market. Recognize how your brand represents your professional identity, values, and unique attributes.

Defining Your Brand Identity: Conduct exercises to define your brand identity, encompassing your core strengths, values, and professional goals. Clarify what sets you apart from others in your field.

Creating a Personal Brand Statement: Craft a concise and impactful statement encapsulating your brand essence. This statement should articulate who you are, what you offer, and the value you bring to potential employers.

Online Presence and Professional Image: Evaluate and enhance your online presence on platforms like LinkedIn, personal websites, or professional portfolios. Ensure consistency in portraying your brand across all platforms.

Showcasing Expertise through Content: Set up a good foundation for yourself as an expert in your field by sharing significant substance. These include articles, blog posts, or presentations highlighting your knowledge and expertise.

Networking and Building Relationships: Utilize networking opportunities to reinforce your brand. Engage in meaningful conversations, contribute insights, and build relationships that align with your brand values.

Receiving and Implementing Feedback: Seek feedback from peers, mentors, or industry professionals regarding your brand presentation. Incorporate constructive feedback to refine and strengthen your brand.

Authenticity and Consistency: Emphasize authenticity in presenting your brand. Ensure consistency in messaging, values, and behavior across all professional interactions.

Proactively shaping your brand creates a unique identity that resonates with potential employers and professional networks. A well-crafted personal brand communicates your value proposition effectively, setting the stage for impactful networking and career advancement opportunities.

CHAPTER 3

OPTIMIZING YOUR RESUME AND INTRODUCTORY LETTER

Creating a convincing resume and introductory letter is crucial in making a solid first impression on potential employers. This chapter provides detailed guidance on optimizing these essential documents to showcase your skills and qualifications effectively.

3.1 RESUME ESSENTIALS:

Understanding Resume Formats: Explore various resume formats (chronological, functional, combination) and choose the most suitable format to highlight your experiences and skills.

Structuring Your Resume: Learn how to organize sections, including contact information, summary or objective, work experience, education, skills, and achievements, to create a clear and impactful resume layout.

Tailoring for Specific Roles: Understand the importance of customizing your resume for each job application. Highlight relevant skills and experiences that match the job description.

Quantifying Achievements: Demonstrate accomplishments using quantifiable metrics or results to emphasize your impact in previous roles.

3.2 CRAFTING A STANDOUT COVER LETTER:

Understanding Cover Letter Purpose: Learn how to craft a compelling cover letter that introduces you, summarizes critical experiences, and expresses your enthusiasm for the position.

Personalizing Your Cover Letter: Tailor cover letters for every application by tending to the employing administrator by name and customizing content to align with the company's values and job requirements.

Showcasing Your Value: Use the cover letter to elaborate on experiences, skills, and achievements not detailed in the resume, highlighting why you are an ideal fit for the role.

Professional Tone and Clarity: Ensure clarity, conciseness, and a professional tone throughout the cover letter, demonstrating your communication skills.

3.3 Online Presence and Application Tracking Systems (Ats):

Optimizing for ATS: Understand how applicant tracking systems work and incorporate relevant keywords and formatting strategies to enhance the chances of your resume passing through these systems.

LinkedIn Profile and Online Consistency: Align your LinkedIn profile with your resume and cover letter. Ensure consistency in professional information, experiences, and skills across all platforms.

This chapter equips job seekers with the tools and strategies to create impactful resumes and cover letters. By mastering these documents, individuals can effectively communicate their skills and socialize in the competitive job market.

Resume Essentials:

Here's a breakdown of the essentials for crafting an effective resume:

1. Contact Information:

Incorporate your name, telephone number, proficient email address, and LinkedIn profile (if applicable) at the top of the resume.

Ensure the information is up-to-date and easily accessible.

2. Summary or Objective Statement:

A brief, compelling summary (for experienced professionals) or an objective statement (for entry-level candidates) highlighting your skills, experience, and career goals.

Tailor this section to match the job you're applying for.

3. Work Experience:

List professional experiences chronologically, starting with your most recent position.

Include job titles, company names, dates of employment, and concise descriptions of responsibilities and achievements for each role.

Use action verbs and quantify achievements where possible to demonstrate impact.

4. Education:

List your educational background, including degrees earned, institution names, graduation dates, and relevant certifications or honors.

For recent graduates or those with limited work experience, education details might precede work experience.

5. Skills:

Include a dedicated section highlighting relevant skills such as technical proficiencies, language abilities, software knowledge, and any specialized skills pertinent to the job.

Separate skills into categories like technical, soft, and certifications for clarity.

6. Achievements and Awards:

Highlight notable achievements, awards, or recognitions earned throughout your career or education relevant to the job you're seeking.

Showcase accomplishments that demonstrate your skills and contributions.

7. Additional Sections (Optional):

Consider including sections like volunteer work, professional affiliations, publications, projects, or interests if they add value to your application or demonstrate relevant skills.

Add sections that strengthen your candidacy and are directly related to the job.

Formatting Tips:

Maintain a clean and professional layout with easily readable fonts and consistent formatting throughout the document.

Use bullet points for readability and keep the resume concise, ideally fitting on one page (unless you have extensive experience).

Customize your resume for every job application, emphasizing relevant experiences and skills.

A well-structured and tailored resume is crucial in presenting yourself as a strong candidate. Adapting these essentials to match your experiences and the job you're applying for can significantly increase your chances of securing an interview.

Crafting a Standout Cover Letter

Creating a standout cover letter is essential to complement your resume and make a compelling case for why you're the ideal candidate for the job. Here's a guide on how to craft an impactful cover letter:

1. Header with Contact Information:

Include your contact information at the top of the cover letter, similar to your resume format.

Date the letter and address it to the hiring manager or specific contact person.

2. Introduction:

Address the recipient by name if known. If not, use a professional greeting such as "Dear Hiring Manager."

Begin with a solid and engaging opening that grabs attention. Consider starting with an exciting fact, mutual connection, or a compelling statement about the company or position.

3. Express Your Interest:

Clearly state the position you're applying for and express your interest in the role and the company.

Explain why you're drawn to the company's mission, values, or specific projects, showing that you've researched and understand the organization.

4. Highlight Your Skills and Experiences:

Expand on a few critical experiences from your resume that directly relate to the job description.

Utilize explicit guides to represent your abilities and accomplishments, demonstrating how your past experiences align with the company's needs.

5. Show Your Fit:

Exhibit how your abilities and encounters make you an optimal fit for the job and how you can add to the organization's prosperity.

Emphasize what you can bring to the company, addressing their needs and challenges.

6. Tailor and Personalize:

Modify each introductory letter for the particular work by highlighting relevant experiences and aligning your qualifications with the job requirements.

Avoid using a generic template; personalize your cover letter to demonstrate your interest in the position.

7. Ending Paragraph:

Repeat your advantage in the position and express gratitude for the opportunity to apply.

I will politely request an interview or meeting to discuss further how you can contribute to the company.

8. Formal Closing:

End the letter professionally with a formal closing, such as "Sincerely," followed by your full name and contact information.

Formatting Tips:

Keep the cover letter concise, typically within one page, and use a precise and professional font.

Edit cautiously to guarantee there are no linguistic errors or typos.

A well-crafted cover letter allows you to present a more personal and engaging story about your qualifications and interest in the job. It should complement your resume and entice the hiring manager to learn more about you as a candidate.

CHAPTER 4

NETWORKING STRATEGIES FOR CAREER SUCCESS

Organizing is an essential part of professional success. Here are some effective strategies for successful networking:

1. Define Your Networking Goals:

Clarify your networking objectives. Determine if you seek job opportunities, industry insights, mentorship, or professional relationships.

Set specific and achievable networking goals to guide your interactions.

2. Utilize Online Platforms:

Leverage networking platforms like LinkedIn to connect with industry professionals, recruiters, and colleagues. Join industry-specific groups and actively engage by sharing insights, participating in discussions, and building connections.

3. Attend Industry Events and Conferences:

Attend seminars, workshops, conferences, and networking events relevant to your field.

Prepare an elevator pitch introducing yourself and your professional goals to initiate conversations.

4. Instructive Interviews:

Demand enlightening meetings with experts in jobs or industries of interest.

Use these meetings to gather insights, seek advice, and expand your network. Show genuine interest and gratitude for their time.

5. Maintain and nurture relationships:

Instead of securing certain advantages, put more effort into establishing trustworthy relationships.

Follow up with contacts, express appreciation, and stay in touch periodically to cultivate lasting connections.

6. Offer Value and Support:

Be willing to assist others in your network by sharing knowledge, providing referrals, or offering support when possible.

Actively contribute to your network's success, fostering a reciprocal relationship.

7. Networking within Your Current Company:

Engage with your organization's colleagues, supervisors, and professionals to expand your internal network.

Participate in company events, cross-departmental collaborations, or affinity groups to build relationships.

8. Elevate Your Online Presence:

Keep an expert and predictable web-based presence across stages.

Share industry-related content, articles, or insights to establish yourself as a knowledgeable and engaged professional.

9. Follow Up and Stay Organized:

Keep track of your networking activities, contacts, and conversations using tools or systems that work for you.

Follow up promptly after meetings or events, expressing appreciation and summarizing key points discussed.

10. Seek Mentorship and Guidance:

Identify potential mentors or advisors within your network and seek guidance from experienced professionals.
A mentor can offer valuable insights, advice, and support for career growth.

Implementing these networking strategies strategically and consistently can significantly expand your professional network, create new opportunities, and contribute to your career advancement and development.

4.1 LEVERAGING PROFESSIONAL PLATFORMS

Leveraging professional platforms is a great way to expand your network and enhance career opportunities. Here's how you can effectively utilize these platforms:

1. LinkedIn:

Create a comprehensive and polished LinkedIn profile showcasing your skills, experiences, and professional accomplishments.

Connect with colleagues, industry professionals, recruiters, and alumni to expand your network.

Share relevant content, articles, or insights in your field to demonstrate expertise and engage with your network.

2. GitHub (for Tech Professionals):

Showcase your coding projects, contributions, and repositories on GitHub to demonstrate your coding skills and expertise.

Engage with other developers, participate in open-source projects, and collaborate to expand your network within the tech community.

3. Behance and Dribbble (for Designers/Creatives):

Display your design portfolio, projects, and creative works on platforms like Behance or Dribble.

Connect with other designers, seek feedback, and engage in discussions to network within the creative industry.

4. ResearchGate or Academia.edu (for Academics/Researchers):

Share academic papers, research findings, and publications on ResearchGate or Academia.edu.

Connect with fellow researchers, academics, and professionals in your field to collaborate and exchange ideas.

5. Professional Forums and Communities:

Participate in industry-specific forums, such as Reddit communities, Quora, or specialized discussions related to your field.

Contribute significant experiences, answer questions, and connect with professionals to establish your expertise.

6. Industry-Specific Platforms:

Explore industry-specific platforms like AngelList for startups, Crunchbase for business and Technology, or ProZ for translators and linguists.

Join relevant groups or communities within these platforms to connect with professionals in your niche industry.

7. Professional Associations and Groups:

Join proficient affiliations or gatherings connected with your industry, both online and offline.

Attend virtual events, webinars, and conferences these associations organize to network and stay updated on industry trends.

8. Online Learning Platforms:

Engage with online learning platforms like Coursera, Udemy, or edX, where you can learn new skills and interact with instructors and peers.

9. Networking through Blogging or Podcasting:

Start a professional blog or podcast discussing topics relevant to your industry.

Engage with your audience, invite guests, and participate in discussions to expand your network within your niche.

10. Maintain Consistency and Professionalism:

Ensure consistency in your profiles across platforms, maintaining a professional tone and effectively showcasing your expertise and accomplishments.

By strategically utilizing these professional platforms, you can broaden your connections, stay updated with industry trends, and discover new career opportunities or collaborations within your field.

4.2 NETWORKING DOS AND DON'TS

Networking involves more than just meeting people; it's about building relationships and fostering professional connections. Here are some networking dos and don'ts to keep in mind:

Networking Dos:

Be Genuine and Authentic: Be yourself and aim for genuine connections. Authenticity builds trust and fosters lasting relationships.

Listen Actively:

1. Practice active listening during conversations.

2. Show interest in others' experiences and perspectives.

3. Engage in meaningful dialogue by asking questions and showing genuine curiosity.

Have a Clear Elevator Pitch: Prepare a concise, engaging pitch introducing yourself and your professional background. Tailor it to different audiences or situations.

Observe and Stay in Touch: Follow up with a thank-you note or email after networking events or meetings. Keep in touch periodically to nurture relationships.

Offer Help and Value: Be ready to offer assistance or support to your connections. Providing value without expecting immediate returns strengthens relationships.

Attend Diverse Events: Participate in various networking events, both industry-specific and general, to expand your network with diverse professionals.

Be Open to New Connections: Don't limit yourself to only networking with people in your field. Valuable connections can come from unexpected places or industries.

Be Professional in Online Interactions: Maintain professionalism in all online interactions and platforms. Use appropriate language and professionally present yourself.

Networking Don'ts:

Don't Be Overly Aggressive: Avoid pushing your agenda too hard or appearing desperate for immediate results. Networking is about building relationships, not immediate gains.

Avoid Being Self-Centered: Focus on mutual conversations and avoid dominating discussions solely about yourself or your achievements.

Don't Dismiss Anyone: Treat everyone respectfully, regardless of their job title or perceived importance. You never know who might offer valuable insights or opportunities.

Avoid Overlooking Follow-Ups: Neglecting to follow up after networking interactions can weaken potential relationships. Send timely and personalized follow-up messages.

Don't Limit Your Networking to Events: Networking involves more than just going to events. Engage in online platforms, professional groups, and informal settings to broaden connections.

Avoid Being Passive in Conversations: Engage actively during discussions. Don't just listen; contribute with relevant insights and thoughtful questions.

Avoid Being Inconsistent or Unreliable: If you promise assistance or follow-up, ensure you deliver. Being inconsistent can damage relationships and your professional reputation.

Don't Forget to Show Gratitude: Always express gratitude for someone's time or help. Failing to acknowledge their efforts can leave a negative impression.

By adhering to these networking dos and avoiding the corresponding don'ts, you'll be better equipped to build meaningful professional connections that can benefit your career growth and development.

4.3 INFORMATIONAL INTERVIEWS AND THEIR IMPACT

Informational interviews are powerful tools for gathering insights, extending your organization, and acquiring a more profound comprehension of industries, roles, or companies. Here's a closer look at their impact and how to conduct them effectively:

Impact of Informational Interviews:

Insights and Industry Knowledge: Informational interviews offer firsthand insights into various industries, job roles, and career paths. They provide a clearer picture of what professionals in specific fields do daily.

Networking Opportunities: They serve as valuable networking opportunities, permitting you to interface with experts, construct connections, and expand your network within your desired industry or company.

Career Guidance and Advice: Professionals you interview can offer valuable advice, guidance, and tips on navigating your career path, providing suggestions for skill development or potential opportunities.

Company Culture Understanding: Informational interviews can provide a glimpse into a company's culture, values, and work environment, giving you a better understanding before applying for a job.

Refinement of Career Goals: These conversations help clarify your career goals and aspirations, allowing you to come to additional educated conclusions about your expert way.

Tips for Conducting Effective Informational Interviews:

Research and Preparation: Before the interview, research the person, background, and the industry or company. Prepare thoughtful questions.

Requesting the Interview: Politely and professionally ask the interviewee via email or LinkedIn, clearly stating your intention and expressing appreciation for their time.

Focus on Learning: During the interview, focus on gathering information rather than asking for a job. Ask open-ended questions about their experiences, challenges, and advice.

Be Respectful of Their Time: Keep the interview concise and within the agreed-upon time frame. Respect their schedule and thank them for their insights.

Follow-Up: Send a card to say thanks or email, offering thanks for their time. Consider updating them on how their advice impacted your decisions or actions.

Maintain Relationships:

1. Stay in touch periodically.
2. Update them on your progress or new achievements.

3. Nurture the relationship for potential future opportunities.

Professionalism: Treat the conversation as a professional meeting. Be courteous, attentive, and prepared to engage in meaningful dialogue.

Informational interviews can greatly benefit career growth, knowledge acquisition, and networking. Approaching them with genuine curiosity, respect, and a willingness to learn can lead to fruitful connections and valuable insights.

CHAPTER 5

UTILIZING ONLINE JOB BOARDS AND RESOURCES

Utilizing online job boards and resources effectively is essential for finding and applying for suitable job opportunities. Here's a guide on how to make the most of these platforms:

1. Identify Reputable Job Boards:

Explore established job boards like LinkedIn, Indeed, Glassdoor, Monster, and specialized industry-specific boards relevant to your field.

2. Create Targeted Profiles:

Build a robust and detailed profile on these platforms, highlighting your skills, experiences, and career objectives.

Use keywords relevant to your desired job to increase visibility in searches.

3. Set Up Job Alerts:

Use job alert features to receive notifications for new job postings that match your criteria.

Fine-tune alerts by specifying job titles, locations, or companies you're interested in.

4. Regularly Review and Apply:

Check job listings frequently and apply promptly to relevant positions. Don't delay applications, as some roles may have deadlines.

5. Tailor Your Applications:

Modify your resume and introductory letter for every application, aligning them with the job description and company requirements.

Highlight critical skills and experiences that match the job posting.

6. Network on Job Platforms:

Engage with professionals, recruiters, and companies on these platforms. Join industry-related groups and participate in discussions.

Connect with recruiters or professionals from companies you're interested in to expand your network.

7. Explore Company Career Pages:

Visit the professional pages of organizations you're keen on. Many organizations post-employment opportunities straightforwardly on their sites.

8. Utilize Advanced Search Filters:

Use advanced search filters on job boards to narrow down job listings based on criteria like location, salary range, experience level, etc.

9. Research Company Reviews:

Use platforms like Glassdoor to research company reviews, employee experiences, and insights into company culture before applying.

10. Follow Application Instructions:

Pay attention to specific application instructions provided by employers. Ensure you follow them meticulously to increase your chances of consideration.

11. Monitor and Track Applications:

Keep track of the positions you've applied to, follow up when necessary, and maintain organized records of your job search activities.

12. Stay Persistent and Positive:

Job searching can be challenging, but persistence pays off. Stay positive, motivated, and resilient throughout the process.

By utilizing online job boards effectively and employing an essential way to deal with your pursuit of employment, you can expand your visibility to potential employers and discover relevant job opportunities that align with your career goals.

5.1 NAVIGATING JOB SEARCH WEBSITES

Navigating job search websites efficiently can significantly enhance your job-seeking experience. Here's a step-by-step guide on how to navigate these platforms effectively:

1. Choose Reliable Job Search Websites:

Opt for reputable job search websites such as LinkedIn, Indeed, Glassdoor, Monster, CareerBuilder, and specific niche job boards relevant to your industry.

2. Create a Profile:

Join and make an itemized profile on the chosen websites. Complete all necessary sections, including work experience, skills, education, and preferences.

3. Use Advanced Search Filters:

Utilize advanced search filters provided by these websites to narrow down job listings. Filter by job title, location, company, salary range, and experience level.

4. Save Customized Job Searches:

Save customized job searches based on your preferences. This allows you to effectively access and survey new job postings that match your criteria.

5. Set Up Job Alerts:

Enable job alerts to receive notifications via email or within the platform whenever new job listings matching your search criteria are posted.

6. Explore Company Pages:

Research and explore company pages within these websites. Many companies post job openings or have dedicated career pages directly on their profiles.

7. Apply Filters Wisely:

Use filters judiciously to avoid limiting your search too much. Experiment with different combinations of filters to cast a broader net while targeting relevant opportunities.

8. Review Job Descriptions Thoroughly:

Read job descriptions carefully to understand each position's requirements, responsibilities, and qualifications. Tailor your applications accordingly.

9. Apply Directly Through the Website:

Apply directly through the job search website whenever possible. Adhere to the application guidelines given by the business.

10. Research Company Insights:

Utilize features on these websites that provide company insights, employee reviews, salary information, and details about company culture to make informed decisions.

11. Network and Engage:

Engage with professionals, recruiters, and companies on these platforms. Join relevant groups, participate in discussions, and network to expand your connections.

12. Review and Manage Applications:

Regularly review your applications, track their status, and follow up if necessary. Keep organized records of your job applications and correspondence.

13. Stay Updated and Persistent:

Visit these sites as often as possible to remain refreshed on new job postings. Persistence is vital in job searching, so apply and network actively.

By effectively following these steps and utilizing the features offered by job search websites, you can streamline your job search process, discover relevant opportunities, and increase your chances of landing interviews for positions that align with your career goals.

5.2 MAKING THE MOST OF ONLINE RESOURCES

Making the most of online resources in your job search involves utilizing various tools and platforms available on the internet. Here's a comprehensive guide on how to maximize online resources:

1. Job Search Platforms:

Utilize reputable job search platforms like LinkedIn, Indeed, Glassdoor, and specialized industry-specific websites. Create detailed profiles and set up job alerts.

2. Professional Networking Sites:

Leverage networking sites like LinkedIn to connect with industry professionals, join groups, and engage in discussions. Build a robust online network.

3. Online Learning Platforms:

Use internet learning stages like Coursera, Udemy, or LinkedIn to learn how to obtain new abilities and accreditations relevant to your field.

4. Company Career Pages:

Visit company career pages to explore job openings directly posted by employers: research company culture, values, and job requirements.

5. Industry-Specific Forums and Groups:

Engage in industry-specific forums, Reddit communities, or specialized groups related to your field. Contribute insights and network with professionals.

6. Resume and Cover Letter Tools:

Use online resume and cover letter builders to create professional and customized documents tailored for different job applications.

7. Portfolio Websites for Creatives:

Make a web-based portfolio utilizing stages like Behance or Dribble to showcase your creative work if you're in design, art, or a creative field.

8. Interview Preparation Resources:

Access interview preparation resources and websites offering tips, sample questions, and mock interview sessions to enhance your interview skills.

9. Research and Company Review Sites:

Use websites like Glassdoor, Vault, or Comparably to research company reviews, salaries, interview experiences, and insights into workplace culture.

10. Professional Associations and Publications:

Join professional associations related to your industry. Access industry-specific publications, articles, and journals available online.

11. Freelancing and Gig Platforms:

Explore freelancing platforms like Upwork, Fiverr, or Freelancer if seeking freelance opportunities or short-term projects.

12. Remote Work Platforms:

Use remote work platforms like Remote. Co, FlexJobs, or We Work Remotely if looking for remote job opportunities.

13. Financial and Career Planning Tools:

Access financial planning tools or career assessment platforms to evaluate your career path and plan your professional development.

14. Government and Non-profit Job Portals:

Check government job portals or non-profit organization websites for job opportunities in the public or non-profit sectors.

15. Online Mentoring or Coaching Platforms:

Seek guidance or mentorship through online mentoring platforms or coaching services tailored to your industry or career goals.

By effectively leveraging these online resources, you can optimize your job search, enhance your skills, grow your organization, and gain vital knowledge to push your career forward.

CHAPTER 6

INTERVIEW PREPARATION AND TECHNIQUES

Here's a comprehensive guide on interview preparation and techniques:

1. Research the Company:

Understand the company's mission, values, products/services, culture, recent news, and critical individuals. Use company websites, news articles, and social media.

2. Understand the Job Description:

Analyze the job description thoroughly. Note the required skills, responsibilities, and qualifications. Prepare specific examples of how your experience aligns with these.

3. Practice Common Interview Questions:

Prepare responses to common interview questions (e.g., strengths/weaknesses, tell me about yourself, why do you want this job) using the STAR method (Situation, Task, Action, Result).

4. Behavioral Interview Preparation:

Be ready for behavioral questions that assess your past experiences and behaviors. Utilize the STAR technique to give organized and compact responses.

5. Mock Interviews:

Conduct mock interviews with friends, family, or mentors to simulate real interview scenarios. Practice your responses and receive constructive feedback.

6. Know Your Resume:

Be familiar with your resume and experiences. Expect questions based on your resume, and prepare to expand on your accomplishments and experiences.

7. Prepare Questions for the Interviewer:

Plan innovative inquiries to pose to the questioner about the role, team dynamics, company culture, or any recent developments in the company.

8. Dress Appropriately:

Dress in proficient clothing that lines up with the company's culture. When in doubt, opt for a conservative and polished appearance.

9. Practice Non-verbal Communication:

Practice confident body language, maintain eye contact, offer a firm handshake, and exhibit active listening skills during the interview.

10. Showcase Your Achievements:

Highlight specific achievements and quantifiable results from your previous experiences to demonstrate your value to the potential employer.

11. Stay Positive and Confident:

Stay positive throughout the interview—project confidence in your abilities without appearing overconfident.

12. Arrive Early and Be Prepared:

Plan to show up sooner than expected for the meeting to stay away from excessive pressure. Bring additional duplicates of your resume, a scratch pad, and a pen.

13. Mind Your Etiquette:

Practice proper interview etiquette, including being courteous to receptionists and interviewers.

14. Follow Up:

Within a day, write a thank-you email expressing gratitude for the open door and reaffirming your interest in the position.

15. Stay Updated with Interview Trends:

Stay informed about the latest interview trends and techniques, including virtual interview etiquette and remote interview best practices.

By preparing thoroughly, practicing, and mastering these interview techniques, you can increase your confidence, showcase your qualifications effectively, and make a strong impression during the interview process.

6.1 RESEARCHING THE COMPANY AND ROLE

Researching the company and the role you're applying for is crucial in preparing for a job interview. Here's a step-by-step guide on how to conduct effective research:

1. Company Website:

Start by thoroughly exploring the company's official website. Look for information about their history, mission, values, products/services, and company culture. Pay attention to any recent news or press releases.

2. Read Annual Reports and Financial Statements:

Review the company's annual reports, financial statements, and investor relations section if available.

This can provide insights into the company's financial health, growth, and plans.

3. Social Media Presence:

Check the company's social media profiles (LinkedIn, Twitter, Facebook, Instagram). Look for updates, announcements, and how they engage with their audience.

4. News and Media Coverage:

Search for recent news articles, blog posts, or press releases about the company. Understand any recent achievements, partnerships, or challenges they might have encountered.

5. Company Reviews:

Check employee reviews on websites like Glassdoor or Indeed to gain insights into the company's work culture, employee experiences, and potential strengths or weaknesses.

6. Understand the Industry:

Research the industry in which the company operates.
Understand market trends, competitors, and any industry
challenges or opportunities.

7. LinkedIn Profiles:

Review the profiles of key individuals within the
company, including executives, department heads, or
individuals in roles similar to the one you're applying for.

8. Job Description Analysis:

Analyze the job description thoroughly. Identify key
responsibilities, required skills, and qualifications. Tailor
your preparation to align your skills and experiences with
the role.

9. Identify Connections:

Identify any personal or professional connections within
the company. Networking or speaking to current or
former employees can provide valuable insights.

10. Prepare Questions:

Based on your research, formulate thoughtful questions
about the company, its culture, future goals, or its role.

Asking well-informed questions during the interview demonstrates your genuine interest.

By conducting comprehensive research on the company and the role, you'll demonstrate your preparedness during the interview and better understand how your skills and experiences align with the company's needs and values. This information will assist you with fitting your reactions and make a stronger impression on the interviewer.

6.2 COMMON INTERVIEW QUESTIONS AND HOW TO ANSWER THEM

Here are some common interview questions and tips on how to approach them:

1. Tell me about yourself.
Approach:

1. Give a concise outline of your expert foundation, relevant experiences, and skills.

    2. Focus on aspects directly related to the job you're applying for.

    3. Emphasize your accomplishments and career goals.

2. What are your strengths?

Approach: Highlight strengths that align with the job description. Provide specific examples or situations where you demonstrated these strengths and the positive outcomes they led to.

3. What are your weaknesses?

Approach:

    1. Discuss a genuine weakness but frame it in a positive light.

    2. Focus on how you're working to improve or overcome this weakness.

    3. Show self-awareness and willingness to learn.

4. Why do you want to work for this company?

Approach:

    1. Demonstrate your knowledge about the company.

2. Discuss specific aspects such as company culture, values, products/services, or recent achievements that attract you.

3. Connect these aspects to your own career goals.

5. Can you describe a challenging situation you faced at work and how you handled it?

Approach: Use the STAR method (Situation, Task, Action, Result) to structure your answer. Describe the challenging situation, your action to address it, as well as the favorable outcome or example gained

6. Where do you see yourself in 5 years?

Approach: Align your answer with the potential career path within the company. Emphasize your ambition, desire for growth, and how you plan to contribute to the company's success.

7. Why should we hire you?

Approach: Highlight your unique skills, experiences, and achievements that make you a perfect fit for the role.

Focus on what you can bring to the company and how to solve its challenges.

8. How do you handle stress or pressure?

Approach: Provide examples of strategies to manage stress, such as time management, prioritization, seeking colleague support, or maintaining a positive attitude. Feature your capacity to keep quiet and centered under tension.

9. Tell me about a time when you had to work in a team.

Approach: Discuss a successful teamwork experience, highlighting your role, contributions, and how you collaborated with others to achieve a common goal. Emphasize communication, problem-solving, and your team-oriented approach.

10. Do you have any questions for us?

Approach: Prepare thoughtful questions demonstrating your interest in the company, the role, or future direction.

Avoid questions that can quickly be answered by researching the company online.

Practice your reactions to these inquiries, guaranteeing that your answers are concisely focused and showcase your qualifications and suitability for the job. Use specific examples and be prepared to adapt your responses based on the interview context.

6.3 MASTERING THE ART OF BEHAVIORAL INTERVIEWS

Conduct interviews centered around previous encounters and behavior methods to predict your performance in future roles. Here's how to excel in behavioral interviews:

1. Understand the STAR Method:

Situation: Depict the unique circumstance or circumstance you were in.

Task: Explain the task or challenge you faced in that situation.

Action: Detail the steps you took to address the task or situation.

Result: Share the outcome of your actions and what you learned from it.

2. Review Common Behavioral Questions:

Practice responses using the STAR method for questions like:

"Tell me about a time when you had to solve a problem."

"Describe a situation where you had to work under pressure."

"Might you at any point examine when you drove a group through a challenging project?"

3. Prepare Specific Examples:

Use diverse examples from various experiences: work, volunteer activities, academics, or extracurricular.

Tailor your examples to highlight skills and qualities relevant to the job description.

4. Be Specific and Quantify Results:

Provide specific details and quantify your achievements wherever possible.

Explain the impact of your actions, such as time saved, revenue generated, or efficiency improved.

5. Stay Structured and Concise:

Stick to the STAR method to maintain a structured response.

Be concise while covering all elements of the situation, task, action, and result.

6. Focus on Your Contributions:

Emphasize your contributions within a team context.

Highlight leadership, problem-solving, communication, and adaptability skills.

7. Use Diverse Examples:

Prepare examples that cover various scenarios: conflicts resolved, projects managed, challenges overcome, or innovations implemented.

8. Practice and Get Feedback:

Lead mock meetings with a companion, relative, or coach.

Seek feedback on your responses to refine your storytelling and ensure clarity.

9. Research the Company's Values:

Align your examples with the company's values or culture, demonstrating how your experiences align with their expectations.

10. Stay Calm and Confident:

Remain composed and confident while sharing your experiences.

If needed, take a moment to gather your thoughts before responding.

11. Be Honest and Authentic:

Be truthful about your experiences and avoid fabricating or exaggerating situations.

Authenticity is critical to building rapport and credibility with the interviewer.

12. Follow-Up with Thank You Notes:

Send a thank-you note after the interview, reiterating your interest and briefly mentioning how you enjoyed discussing your experiences.

By preparing thoroughly, practicing storytelling using the STAR method, and tailoring your examples to showcase relevant skills, you'll effectively demonstrate your capabilities and suitability for the role during a behavioral interview.

CHAPTER 7

NEGOTIATING JOB OFFERS AND EVALUATING OPPORTUNITIES

Negotiating job offers and evaluating opportunities is crucial in securing a position that aligns with your career goals and compensation expectations. Here are steps to effectively navigate this process:

1. Understand Your Value:

Research industry standards, market rates, and the value of your skills and experience. Websites such as Glassdoor and Salary.com can provide salary information. Salary benchmarks.

2. Consider the Entire Offer:

Evaluate the compensation package, including salary, bonuses, benefits, stock options, vacation time, retirement plans, and other perks.

3. Priorities Your Needs:

Identify your priorities regarding compensation, career growth, work-life balance, job responsibilities, company culture, and location.

4. Negotiate from a Position of Strength:

Express enthusiasm and gratitude for the job offer. Wait for the right time to negotiate, usually after receiving a formal request.

5. Prepare Your Negotiation Points:

Be ready to articulate why you're worth the compensation you're requesting. Highlight relevant skills, experiences, and achievements.

6. Request Time for Consideration:

Ask for time to evaluate the offer. This lets you carefully consider the terms and prepare for negotiation without rushing.

7. Be Professional and Courteous:

Keep your negotiation professional, polite, and respectful. Focus on collaboration rather than confrontation.

8. Aim for Win-Win Scenarios:

Seek outcomes that benefit both you and the employer. Be flexible and open to compromise while aiming for an agreement that meets your needs.

9. Consider Non-Monetary Factors:

If the salary isn't negotiable, negotiate other aspects such as additional days off, the option to work remotely, professional development opportunities, or a flexible schedule.

10. Get It in Writing:

Following the conclusion of negotiations, ensure that all terms are included in the job offer letter or contract. Review it carefully before signing.

11. Evaluate the Long-Term Impact:

Consider the long-term implications of the role on your career progression, skill development, and overall satisfaction.

12. Trust Your Instincts:

Trust your instincts if something doesn't feel right or align with your goals. Sometimes, the best decision is turning down an offer that doesn't meet your criteria.

13. Seek Advice if Needed:

Consult mentors, career advisors, or trusted colleagues for guidance if you need clarification on certain aspects of the offer or negotiation process.

14. Keep the Big Picture in Mind:

Look beyond immediate compensation. Consider the potential for growth, learning opportunities, company stability, and alignment with your career aspirations. Negotiating job offers and evaluating opportunities requires a strategic approach that balances your professional worth, career goals, and personal priorities. Approach the negotiation process with confidence, preparedness, and a clear understanding of what you're seeking in your next career move.

7.1 ASSESSING COMPENSATION PACKAGES

Assessing compensation packages involves evaluating various components beyond just the salary. Here's a comprehensive approach to determining a compensation package:

1. Base Salary:

Assess the base salary offered and compare it to industry standards and your expectations based on your experience, skills, and living costs in the job location.

2. Bonuses and Incentives:

Consider performance-based bonuses, signing bonuses, annual incentives, or profit-sharing plans offered by the employer. Understand the criteria for eligibility and payouts.

3. Stock Options or Equity Grants:

Evaluate the value of stock options, restricted stock units (RSUs), or equity grants provided. Understand vesting schedules, potential future value, and tax implications.

4. Benefits Package:

Review the benefits package, including health insurance, dental and vision coverage, retirement plans (401(k)), life insurance, disability benefits, and other perks like gym memberships or commuter benefits.

5. Paid Time Off (PTO) and Vacation Days:

Assess the offered vacation days, paid holidays, sick leave, and any flexibility in scheduling or remote work options.

6. Employee Stock Purchase Plans (ESPPs):

Evaluate if the company offers an ESPP, allowing workers to buy stock at a limited rate. Understand the terms and potential benefits.

7. Education or Tuition Reimbursement:

Consider if the company provides opportunities for educational development or tuition reimbursement for pursuing further education or certifications.

8. Professional Development and Training:

Assess the availability of opportunities for skill development, training programs, workshops, or conferences funded by the employer.

9. Relocation Assistance:

If applicable, evaluate any relocation assistance, such as moving allowances, temporary housing, or assistance selling/buying a home.

10. Flexibility and Work-Life Balance:

Consider flexible work hours, remote work options, parental leave policies, and other benefits contributing to a healthy work-life balance.

11. Cost of Living Adjustment (COLA):

Inquire about cost of living adjustments if the job requires relocation to a higher-cost area.

12. Company Culture and Perks:

Assess intangible benefits such as company culture, opportunities for growth, mentorship programs, employee discounts, or other unique perks.

13. Comprehensive Evaluation:

Evaluate the entire compensation package holistically, considering not only the monetary aspects but also the long-term career prospects, job satisfaction, and alignment with your values and goals.

14. Seek Clarification:

If any aspect of the compensation package is unclear, seek clarification from the employer or HR representative before deciding.

By thoroughly assessing these components and considering both monetary and non-monetary aspects, you can make an informed decision regarding a compensation package that aligns with your career aspirations, financial needs, and work-life balance preferences.

7.2 NEGOTIATION STRATEGIES FOR SUCCESS

Negotiation is crucial, especially when navigating job offers or business-related discussions. Here are effective negotiation strategies for success:

1. Research and Preparation:

Research industry standards, market rates, and comparable salaries for similar positions. Be clear about your value and what you're aiming for.

2. Priorities Goals and Understand Limits:

Define your priorities and must-haves in the negotiation. Understand your bottom line and the aspects where you can be flexible.

3. Focus on Mutual Gains:

Hold back nothing to ensure a victory where both players benefit. Emphasize how your skills and contributions will bring value to the employer while achieving your goals.

4. Build Rapport and Establish Trust:

Foster a positive relationship with the other party. Listen actively, show empathy, and maintain professionalism to build trust during the negotiation.

5. Let the Other Party Make the First Offer:

Encourage the employer to state the initial offer. This enables you to verify their claims and bargain from a more informed position.

6. Present Your Case Effectively:

Clearly articulate your values, skills, experiences, and achievements that justify the compensation you're seeking. Use concrete examples to support your claims.

7. Negotiate Beyond Salary:

Explore other aspects of the compensation package. Consider benefits, bonuses, stock options, flexible hours, professional development, or additional perks.

8. Be Patient and Flexible:

Maintain patience during negotiations. Be willing to listen and consider alternative proposals or compromises that meet your employer's needs.

9. Use Positive Language and Tone:

Use positive and collaborative language throughout the negotiation. Frame your requests as opportunities for mutual success rather than demands.

10. Practice Active Listening:

Listen attentively to the employer's responses and concerns. Address their points thoughtfully, showing that you understand and respect their perspective.

11. Don't Rush to Accept:

Take time to evaluate offers and counteroffers. Avoid making impulsive decisions; asking for time to consider the request thoroughly is okay.

12. Consider Walking Away if Necessary:

Be prepared to walk away if the offer aligns differently from your priorities or negotiations are impasse. This can sometimes lead to a better offer or alternative opportunities.

13. Get Agreements in Writing:

As soon as an agreement is reached, ensure all agreed terms are recorded in writing to avoid misunderstandings.

14. Remain Professional and Gracious:

Regardless of the outcome, maintain professionalism and gratitude for the opportunity to negotiate. Future opportunities arise from a favorable impression. Effective negotiation involves strategic planning, effective communication, and flexibility. These techniques allow you to investigate talks efficiently and accomplish results that line up with your objectives and priorities.

CHAPTER 8

MAINTAINING PROFESSIONALISM AND ETHICS IN JOB SEARCH

Maintaining professionalism and ethics throughout the job search process is essential for building a positive reputation and ensuring a successful career transition. Here are fundamental principles to uphold:

1. Honesty and Integrity:

Be truthful and transparent in your job application materials, resume, cover letter, and interviews. Avoid misrepresenting your skills or experiences.

2. Respectful Communication:

Use professional language and tone in all communications, whether written (emails, cover letters) or verbal (phone calls, interviews). Treat everyone respectfully, from recruiters to potential employers.

3. Confidentiality and Discretion:

Respect confidentiality, mainly if you're currently employed. Avoid discussing sensitive information about your current job or employer during interviews or networking.

4. Professional Online Presence:

Retain a professional image through streaming platforms like LinkedIn, ensuring your profiles are up-to-date and showcasing relevant skills and experiences. Avoid posting controversial or unprofessional content.

5. Timely Responses and Follow-Ups:

Respond promptly to emails, calls, or interview invitations. Send thank-you notes or emails after interviews to express gratitude and reiterate your interest in the position.

6. Ethical Networking:

Build relationships through ethical networking. Offer help, share insights, and seek guidance without expecting immediate benefits. Networking should be mutually beneficial.

7. Respect for Competition:

Avoid speaking negatively about competitors or former employers during interviews or networking conversations. Focus on discussing your own experiences and contributions positively.

8. Adherence to Company Policies:

When interviewing or negotiating job offers, respect the policies and procedures set by both your current and potential employers.

9. Avoiding Conflicts of Interest:

Be mindful of conflicts of interest. Refrain from using proprietary information from your current employer in job applications or interviews with competitors.

10. Ethical Decision-Making:

Make ethical choices throughout the job search process, especially when considering multiple offers. Consider the impact on your career, integrity, and values.

11. Honoring Commitments:

Once you accept a job offer, honor your commitment and notify your current employer properly. Avoid reneging on accepted offers unless necessary.

12. Seeking Guidance and Feedback:

Seek guidance from mentors, career advisors, or HR professionals if uncertain about ethical dilemmas during the job search. Welcome constructive feedback. Upholding professionalism and ethics throughout the job search demonstrates your integrity, reliability, and commitment to ethical conduct. It helps build a positive reputation in your industry and contributes to a successful and fulfilling career trajectory.

8.1 ETHICAL JOB SEARCH PRACTICES

Engaging in ethical job search practices is crucial for maintaining your integrity, reputation, and professionalism throughout the job-seeking process. Here are some ethical guidelines to follow:

1. Honesty in Representation:

Present accurate and truthful information on your resume and cover letter during interviews. Avoid exaggerating qualifications or experiences.

2. Respect Confidentiality:

Maintain confidentiality regarding sensitive information about your current employer or colleagues. Refrain from disclosing proprietary information during interviews or networking.

3. Equal Treatment and Fairness:

Treat all potential employers, recruiters, and contacts fairly and equally. Stay away from separation in view of race, orientation, age, religion, or other characteristics.

4. Transparent Communication:

Communicate openly and transparently with potential employers. If you have multiple job offers or are considering other opportunities, communicate this respectfully and honestly.

5. Respect for Company Policies:

Adhere to company policies, especially during the interview process. Respect non-disclosure agreements, non-compete clauses, or any other contractual obligations.

6. Avoiding Conflicts of Interest:

Remain clear of situations that could lead to disputes between your current and prospective employers. Refrain from using company time or resources for job search activities.

7. Proper Use of Information:

Use information obtained during interviews or networking responsibly. Avoid sharing proprietary or sensitive details about a company or industry without proper authorization.

8. Ethical Networking Practices:

Engage in networking to build mutually beneficial relationships. Respect others' time, expertise, and boundaries while networking.

9. Considerate Job Offer Considerations:

When considering job offers, weigh the pros and cons ethically. Avoid using a suggestion solely for leverage without genuine interest in the position.

10. Honoring Commitments:

Once you've accepted a job offer, honor your commitment and notify your current employer properly. Avoid reneging on accepted offers unless it's unavoidable.

11. Seek Clarification and Feedback:

Seek clarification on any unclear ethical situations or dilemmas—welcome feedback and guidance from mentors, advisors, or HR professionals.

12. Ethical Behavior in Negotiations:

Negotiate in good faith. Be reasonable, honest, and transparent in discussing compensation, benefits, or job responsibilities.

Adhering to these ethical guidelines demonstrates integrity, professionalism, and reliability, contributing to a positive reputation within your professional network and ensuring a sound foundation for your career growth.

8.2 HANDLING REJECTIONS AND MOVING FORWARD

Dealing with job rejections can be challenging, but it's essential to handle them professionally and use them as opportunities for growth. Here's how to navigate rejections and move forward:

1. Accept Emotions and Reflect:

Allow yourself to acknowledge and process your feelings of disappointment or frustration. Reflect on the rejection to understand if there are areas for improvement.

2. Seek Feedback:

If possible, politely ask for feedback from the employer regarding why you weren't selected. Use this feedback constructively to enhance your skills or approach for future applications.

3. Stay Positive and Maintain Perspective:

Maintain a positive outlook and understand that rejections are a normal part of the job search process. Keep in mind that one rejection does not define one's worth or capabilities.

4. Learn and Adapt:

Use the rejection as a learning experience. Identify areas to improve, whether enhancing specific skills or refining your interview techniques.

5. Stay Resilient and Persistent:

Remain resilient in your job search. Stay persistent and apply to roles that align with your skills and interests.

6. Network and Expand Connections:

Engage in networking activities, attend industry events, and connect with professionals in your field. Significant opportunities and new avenues can arise from systems administration. Insights.

7. Refine Your Application Materials:

Review and refine your resume, cover letter, and online profiles. Tailor them to better highlight your strengths and experiences.

8. Consider Additional Skills or Education:

Consider acquiring new skills or further education that could enhance your qualifications and make you more competitive in the job market.

9. Maintain a Routine and Stay Healthy:

Stick to a routine that includes job searching, networking, and self-care. Dealing with your physical and mental prosperity is crucial during this time.

10. Keep Moving Forward:

Focus on moving forward rather than dwelling on rejections. Use each experience as a stepping stone towards finding the right opportunity.

11. Explore Alternative Paths:

Be open to exploring alternative career paths, freelance work, temporary positions, or volunteer opportunities that may provide valuable experience and connections.

12. Celebrate Achievements and Progress:

Acknowledge and celebrate small victories and progress made during your job search. Each step forward, regardless of its size, is an accomplishment.

Remember that rejection is a natural part of the job search process and doesn't define your worth or abilities. Use it as a catalyst for growth, stay determined, and maintain a positive mindset as you continue your job search journey.

CHAPTER 9

ADAPTING TO CHANGES IN THE EMPLOYMENT LANDSCAPE

Adapting to changes in the employment landscape is pivotal to remaining applicable and cutthroat in your vocation. Here are strategies to navigate shifts in the job market:

1. Continuous Learning and Skill Development:
Keep abreast on shifts in the industry and acquire new skills. through online courses, workshops, certifications, or formal education. Adaptability is key in a rapidly changing job market.

2. Flexibility and Adaptability:
Be open to diverse job opportunities, including remote work, freelance gigs, or part-time roles. Flexibility in your career approach can provide stability in changing times.

3. Networking and Building Relationships:

Extend your expert organization by going to industry occasions, joining online forums, and nurturing connections. Networking can uncover new opportunities and insights.

4. Embrace Technology:

Develop proficiency in relevant technology tools and software used in your field. Tech skills are increasingly valuable across various industries.

5. Enhance Remote Work Competence:

Improve your ability to work remotely efficiently. This includes mastering virtual collaboration tools, effective communication, time management, and creating a conducive home workspace.

6. Entrepreneurial Mindset:

Cultivate an entrepreneurial mindset by seeking innovative solutions, embracing change, and proactively identifying opportunities.

7. Stay Informed and Agile:

Keep yourself updated on market trends, economic shifts, and changes in your industry. Be ready to adapt your skills or pivot your career path accordingly.

8. Resilience and Adaptation:

Develop resilience to cope with uncertainties. If necessary, be prepared to adapt to new work environments, job roles, or industries.

9. Reevaluate and Reinvent:

Periodically reassess your career goals and strategies. Be willing to pivot or reinvent your career path based on changing market demands or personal aspirations.

10. Personal Branding and Online Presence:

Maintain a strong online presence through LinkedIn, personal websites, or professional portfolios. Showcase your skills, achievements, and expertise to attract potential opportunities.

11. Seek Mentorship and Guidance:

Connect with mentors or industry experts who can offer guidance and advice as you navigate changes in the job market.

12. Adapt Emotional Intelligence Skills:

Enhance your emotional intelligence to effectively manage stress, communicate with others, and adapt to various work environments and team dynamics.

Adapting to changes in the employment scene requires a proactive methodology, constant learning, and a readiness to embrace new opportunities. You can thrive in evolving work environments and remain competitive by staying agile and flexible and continuously improving your skills.

9.1 REMOTE WORK AND ITS IMPLICATIONS

Remote work has transformed how people approach their careers and the dynamics of the modern workforce. Here are the implications and key aspects of remote work:

1. Work Flexibility:

Remote work offers increased flexibility, allowing individuals to create their schedules and work from locations of their choice, eliminating the need for a traditional office space.

2. Work-Life Balance:

Remote work can improve work-life balance by reducing commuting time and providing more flexibility to manage personal commitments alongside professional responsibilities.

3. Increased Productivity:

Many remote workers report higher productivity levels due to fewer workplace distractions, personalized work environments, and the ability to structure their day according to their preferences.

4. Global Talent Pool:

Managers can get to a more extensive ability pool by hiring remote workers from diverse locations. This allows for increased diversity and access to specialized skills.

5. Cost Savings:

The two managers and representatives can encounter cost investment funds related to office space, commuting expenses, and other overheads associated with traditional office settings.

6. Technology and Remote Collaboration:

Advancements in Technology have enabled seamless remote collaboration through video conferencing, project management tools, and communication platforms, fostering effective teamwork regardless of physical location.

7. Employee Satisfaction and Retention:

Remote work options often contribute to higher employee satisfaction, leading to increased retention rates. Employees value the flexibility and autonomy offered by remote setups.

8. Challenges of Remote Work:

Remote work poses challenges related to sensations of confinement, trouble isolating work and individual life, and the requirement for strong self-discipline and time management skills.

9. Evolving Company Cultures:

Companies are adapting their cultures to accommodate remote work, focusing on communication, trust-building, and providing adequate support for remote employees.

10. Impact on Real Estate and Infrastructure:

Remote work trends influence real estate markets, reducing demand for office spaces in some areas while potentially driving growth in suburban or rural regions.

11. Legal and Compliance Considerations:

Remote work raises legal considerations such as tax implications, labor laws compliance across different regions or countries, and data security and privacy concerns.

12. Future of Work Models:

Remote work has prompted discussions about hybrid work models that combine remote and in-person work, offering the best of both worlds for employees and employers.

As remote work evolves, employers and employees must adapt to its challenges and opportunities. Creating efficient remote work practices, fostering strong communication, and providing necessary support are crucial for maximizing the benefits of remote work arrangements.

9.2 UPSKILLING AND LIFELONG LEARNING

Upskilling and lifelong learning are critical in today's rapidly evolving job market. Continuous learning helps individuals stay competitive, adaptable, and relevant in their careers. Here are the key aspects and benefits of upskilling and lifelong learning:

1. Adaptation to Technological Advancements: Technology is constantly evolving, impacting various industries. Upskilling allows individuals to stay updated with new tools, software, and emerging technologies relevant to their field.

2. Career Advancement Opportunities:

New abilities or affirmations can open ways to promotions, career transitions, or higher-paying roles. Continuous learning enhances your skill set, making you a more valuable asset.

3. Improved Job Performance:

Upskilling equips you with the latest knowledge and techniques, enhancing your job performance and productivity. It allows you to contribute more effectively to your organization's goals.

4. Enhanced Employability:

Ceaseless learning exhibits your obligation to development and improvement, making you more attractive to employers seeking proactive, adaptable, and skilled individuals.

5. Future-proofing Your Career:

Lifelong learning helps future-proof your career by preparing you for changes in the job market, such as automation, new job roles, or industry shifts.

6. Personal Development and Fulfillment:

Learning new skills fosters personal growth, boosts confidence, and provides a sense of accomplishment, contributing to overall satisfaction and fulfilment.

7. Access to Diverse Opportunities:

Continuous learning expands your knowledge base and skill repertoire, allowing you to explore diverse job opportunities within and outside your current field.

8. Flexibility and Adaptability:

Lifelong learning cultivates a flexible mindset, enabling you to adjust to evolving conditions, take on new difficulties, and learn from experiences.

9. Online Learning Platforms and Resources:

Accessible online learning platforms like Coursera, Udemy, LinkedIn Learning, and others offer various courses, allowing for convenient and flexible learning opportunities.

10. Networking and Knowledge Sharing:

Engaging in learning communities, workshops, or industry events facilitates networking, collaboration, and knowledge sharing with peers, experts, and mentors.

11. Tailoring Learning to Career Goals:

Focus on learning skills that align with your career goals, industry trends, or the direction you wish to take in your profession.

12. Time Management and Consistency:

Establish a routine for learning, allocating dedicated time regularly to upskill. Consistency in learning efforts is crucial for continuous improvement.

Investing in upskilling and lifelong learning is an ongoing process that offers numerous benefits for personal and professional growth. It empowers individuals to adapt, thrive, and remain relevant in a rapidly changing workforce.

9.3 NAVIGATING CAREER TRANSITIONS

Navigating career transitions can be both challenging and rewarding. Whether you're switching industries, changing job roles, or pursuing a new career path, here's a guide to help you successfully navigate these transitions:

1. Self-Assessment:

Evaluate your skills, strengths, weaknesses, interests, and values. Identify what you enjoy and where your passions lie to align with potential career options.

2. Research and Exploration:

Research different career paths, industries, and job roles that match your skills and interests. Explore online resources, attend workshops, and seek informational interviews to gain insights.

3. Identify Transferable Skills:

Recognize skills from your current or past roles that are transferable to your desired career. Feature these abilities in your resume and during meetings to showcase your versatility.

4. Networking and Informational Interviews:

Connect with professionals in your target industry or field. Direct instructive meetings to study the industry, gain advice, and expand your network.

5. Acquire Necessary Skills or Education:

Consider acquiring additional skills, certifications, or formal education if required for your desired career transition. This may involve online courses, workshops, or degree programs.

6. Tailor Your Resume and Cover Letter:

Modify your resume and introductory letter to feature important encounters and abilities that exhibit your appropriateness for the new role or industry.

7. Showcase Adaptability and Flexibility:

Emphasize your adaptability, willingness to learn, and ability to thrive in diverse environments. Managers esteem competitors who can adjust rapidly to new challenges.

8. Be Open to Entry-Level Positions:

Be open to starting at an entry-level position if necessary. It tends to be a venturing stone to acquire experience and establish yourself in a new field or industry.

9. Seek Mentorship and Guidance:

Find mentors or career advisors who can give direction, backing, and bits of knowledge in view of their encounters navigating similar career transitions.

10. Stay Persistent and Patient:

Understand that career transitions might take time. Stay persistent, patient, and proactive in your job search or learning efforts.

11. Embrace Continuous Learning:

Embrace an outlook of nonstop learning and improvement. Remain refreshed on industry patterns, attend workshops, and seek opportunities for skill development.

12. Evaluate and Adjust:

Occasionally evaluate your headway and make vital changes in accordance with your strategy if things aren't progressing as planned. Adaptability is key in navigating career transitions.

Career transitions require determination, flexibility, and a willingness to leave your comfort zone. Take pleasure in the journey, stay focused on your goals, and leverage your experiences and skills to transition into a new and fulfilling career path successfully.

CONCLUSION

In the conclusion of the book "Search Responsibly: The Employment Seeker's Handbook," it's essential to summarize critical points while leaving the reader with a sense of empowerment and guidance. Here's an example of how the conclusion might be crafted:

In conclusion, the journey of employment seeking is not just about finding a job; it's a profound exploration of self-discovery and growth. Throughout this handbook, we've delved into crucial aspects of the job search process, from understanding the modern job market to mastering the art of interviews and navigating career transitions.

Remember, your career path is unique, and each step you take, every skill you acquire, and every connection you make contributes to your personal and professional growth. Embrace the process, stay resilient in the face of challenges, and remain adaptable to changes in the ever-evolving job landscape.

As you navigate your career journey, remember the importance of continuous learning, networking, and self-reflection. Your ability to adapt, learn, and showcase your strengths will set you apart in pursuing professional fulfilment.

Pursuing your ideal career might be challenging, but the amalgamation of experiences, failures, and triumphs shapes your story. Stay true to your aspirations, believe in your capabilities, and remain open to new opportunities that may lead you to unexpected paths.

Lastly, I encourage you to apply the knowledge gained from this handbook, but more importantly, use it with sincerity, integrity, and responsibility. Your journey toward finding meaningful employment is about the objective as well as the illustrations learned and the growth achieved along the way.

Thank you for allowing this handbook to be part of your journey. I wish you the very best in your endeavors.

The conclusion should encapsulate the book's essence, providing a sense of closure while motivating and inspiring readers to apply the knowledge gained as they progress on their employment-seeking journey.

APPENDIX

Additional Resources

The appendix provides supplementary materials and resources to enhance the reader's understanding and practical application of the book's content. It is a valuable reference section to support readers on their employment-seeking journey.

Useful Websites and Online Platforms:

List of reputable job search websites, professional networking platforms, and online resources for skill development, such as LinkedIn, Indeed, Glassdoor, Coursera, and others.

Recommended Reading List:

A curated list of books, articles, or publications related to career development, interview techniques, resume writing, and personal growth.

Templates and Samples:

Sample resumes, cover letters, thank-you notes, and interview preparation guides to assist readers in crafting their application materials effectively.

Career Assessment Tools:

Links to online career assessment tools or quizzes to assist people with surveying their abilities, interests, and personality traits, aiding in career exploration.

Professional Organizations and Associations:

Directory of relevant professional organizations or associations in various industries that offer networking opportunities, industry insights, and career advancement resources.

Further Learning Resources:

Reputable institutions or industry experts offer additional courses, webinars, podcasts, or workshops that delve deeper into specific career-related topics.

Glossary of Terms:

Definitions and explanations of industry-specific terms, acronyms, or jargon are mentioned throughout the book for readers' reference.

Acknowledgements:

A section acknowledging contributors, individuals, or organizations that provided valuable insights, support, or resources during the creation of the handbook.

SAMPLE RESUMES AND COVER LETTERS

Below are sample templates for a resume and a cover letter that could be included in an appendix section of a career handbook:

Sample Resume Template:

[Your Name] [Your Address] [City, State, Zip] [Phone Number] [Email Address]

Objective: [Optional - Briefly state your career objective or professional summary]

Education:

Degree: [Degree Name]

Major: [Your Major]

Institution: [University/College Name]

Graduation Year: [Year]

Experience:

Job Title: [Your Position]

Company Name: [Company/Organization Name]

Dates: [Month/Year - Month/Year]

Responsibilities: [List key responsibilities and achievements using bullet points]

Job Title: [Your Position]

Company Name: [Company/Organization Name]

Dates: [Month/Year - Month/Year]

Responsibilities: [List key responsibilities and achievements using bullet points]

Skills:

Technical Skills: [e.g., Programming Languages, Software Proficiency]

Soft Skills: [e.g., Communication, Leadership]

Language Skills: [e.g., Proficient in Languages]

Certifications:

Certification Name: [Name of Certification]

Issuing Organization: [Issuing Body]

Date Obtained: [Date]

Sample Cover Letter Template:

[Your Name] [Your Address] [City, State, Zip] [Phone Number] [Email Address]

[Date]

[Recruiting Supervisor's Name] [Company Name]

[Company Address] [City, State, Zip]

Dear [Hiring Chief's Name],

I'm writing to communicate my advantage in the [Job Title] position at [Company Name], as promoted. With a solid foundation in [relevant abilities/experience], I'm amped up for the chance to add to [specific venture or part of the company].

In my past job at [Previous Company], I effectively [highlight an accomplishment or obligation applicable to the gig you're applying for]. This experience furnished me with [mention an expertise or knowledge], which would be significant in the [Job Title] job at [Company Name].

Also, I'm enthusiastic about [mention an interest or part of the industry] and am anxious to apply my abilities to add to [Company Name] 's mission of [mention the organization's central goal or values].

Attached is my resume, which further diagrams my capabilities. I'm energetic about joining [Company Name] and adding to its prosperity.

Much obliged to you for thinking about my application. I'm anticipating the amazing chance to talk about how my abilities line up with the requirements of [Company Name].

Warm respects,

[Your Name]

These sample templates serve as a starting point for individuals looking to craft their resumes and cover letters, providing a clear structure and format to showcase their qualifications and enthusiasm for a particular job.

Additional Resources for Further Reading

Providing a list of additional resources for further reading can be immensely helpful for individuals seeking more in-depth information or varied perspectives on career-related topics. Here's a suggested list:

Recommended Reading List:

"What Color Is Your Parachute?" by Richard N. Bolles: A classic career guide covering job-search strategies, career exploration, and finding meaningful work.

"The 7 Habits of Highly Effective People" by Stephen R. Covey: Offers timeless principles for personal and professional effectiveness, focusing on habits that lead to success.

"Lean in: Women, Work, and the Will to Lead" by Sheryl Sandberg: Explores challenges women face in the workplace and provides insights on leadership, career advancement, and achieving goals.

"Drive: The Surprising Truth About What Motivates Us" by Daniel H. Pink: Examines motivation, autonomy, and the science behind what drives individuals to excel in their careers.

"Designing Your Life: How to Build a Well-Lived, Joyful Life" by Bill Burnett and Dave Evans: Guides readers through applying design thinking principles to craft a fulfilling and purposeful career and life.

"StrengthsFinder 2.0" by Tom Rath: Utilizes a strengths-based approach to help individuals identify and maximize their unique talents for career success.

"Emotional Intelligence 2.0" by Travis Bradberry and Jean Greaves: Explores the importance of emotional intelligence in professional success and provides strategies for developing EQ.

"The Startup of You: Adapt to the Future, Invest in Yourself, and Transform Your Career" by Reid Hoffman and Ben Casnocha: Offers strategies for managing your career as if it were a startup, emphasizing adaptability and continuous learning.

"Never Eat Alone: And Other Secrets to Success, One Relationship at a Time" by Keith Ferrazzi: Focuses on the power of networking and building relationships for career advancement.

"Atomic Habits: An Easy & Proven Way to Build Good Habits & Break Bad Ones" by James Clear: Investigates the study of propensity arrangement and how little changes can lead to significant career improvements.

This reading list covers various aspects of career development, personal growth, leadership, and effective habits. It caters to individuals looking to expand their knowledge and gain insights from different perspectives to enhance their careers.

GLOSSARY OF KEY TERMS

Curriculum Vitae (CV): A comprehensive document detailing an individual's academic and professional history, often used in academia and certain industries.

Cover Letter: A document accompanying a resume that introduces the applicant to a potential employer and highlights qualifications and interest in a specific job.

Networking: Constructing and keeping up with proficient connections for professional success, job opportunities, and mutual support.

Soft Skills: Personal attributes, communication abilities, and emotional intelligence that contribute to effective work performance, such as teamwork, adaptability, and leadership.

Hard Skills: Specific, teachable abilities or technical knowledge required for a particular job, such as programming languages, accounting, or project management.

Interview: A gathering between a task candidate and a business to assess qualifications, skills, and suitability for a job position.

Remote Work: Employment arrangement allowing individuals to work from a location other than a traditional office, often using digital technologies to communicate and collaborate.

Career Development: The deep-rooted course of overseeing learning, work, recreation, and advances to move toward a personally determined and evolving preferred future.

Professional Development: Activities designed to enhance professional knowledge, skills, and abilities in one's field or occupation.

Job Search Strategies: Methods and techniques employed to find employment opportunities, including networking, online job boards, recruiters, and direct applications.

Resume: A concise document summarizing an individual's skills, experiences, and education relevant to a job application.

Elevator Pitch: A brief, persuasive speech to introduce oneself professionally, typically in the time it takes to ride an elevator, used in networking or interviews.

LinkedIn: A professional social networking platform for professional networking, job searching, career development, etc.

Career Assessment: Tools or tests used to evaluate an individual's interests, skills, values, and personality traits to assist in career decision-making.

Negotiation: Discussing terms, conditions, or agreements between parties to reach a mutually acceptable arrangement.

www.ingramcontent.com/pod-product-compliance
Lightning Source LLC
Chambersburg PA
CBHW062323290526
45794CB00005B/1870